A Little Book about the Runes

Björn Jónasson

A LITTLE BOOK ABOUT THE

RUNES

GUDRUN

A Little Book about the Runes © GUDRUN 2001 and Björn Jónasson

www.gudrunpublishing.com

English translation © Bernard Scudder and Björn Jónasson

Design and layout: Helgi Hilmarsson, Elísabet Guðbjörnsdóttir and Björn Jónasson

First printing 2001
Second printing 2003

Assistance, good advice and proofreading: Professor Jan Ragnar Hagland, University of Trondheim; Professor Kristján Árnason, University of Iceland; Guðrún Þórhallsdóttir, senior lecturer, University of Iceland; Margrét Eggertsdóttir, researcher, the Arnamagnaen Institute, Copenhagen; Guðbjörn Sigurmundsson, BA; Þórgunnur Snædal, researcher, University of Uppsala.

ISBN 9979-856-38-6

Printed in Iceland
by Oddi Ltd. Printing Press
www.oddi.is

Contents

Rune stone (Uppland, Sweden)

Preface

The aim of this little book is to provide some insight into the world of the runes, the old Germanic alphabet. It was the vikings who made the runes famous. Wherever the vikings went, the runes were part of their luggage.

Much research has been conducted in the past to uncover the mysteries of runes. And much new light has been shed on the runes and their use. The last fifty years have been particularly fruitful in this respect, headed by the large and surprising archaeological finds in Bergen in 1956, which had a great effect on runologists' ideas about the importance of runes in people's everyday lives and dealings.

To make the runes accessible to ordinary readers today, we have used a tried and tested method. They are explained one at a time, with the help of an old poem. This poem or riddle, as many people would like to call it, is found in many old manuscripts and exists in many versions. Its origins are thought to lie in the viking age. The poem is written in the enigmatic style of old Norse poetry, using "kennings" or descriptive metaphors. Each rune is named or referred to in several different ways. So in order to remember the name, you must learn the poem and solve the riddles, and eventually you learn the entire runic alphabet.

The text in this book is a new translation, based on the published version by Bruce Dickins and incorporating some of the amendments and new readings in R.I. Page's recent edition.

Rune stone (Uppland, Sweden)

Introduction

These are the Runes

The old runic alphabet is today usually called the futhark after the first six runes, just as we call our modern alphabet after the first two letters in the Greek alphabet, alpha and beta. A number of variants of the futhark (or futhork) exist, and the same goes for many of the runes.

The runic alphabet used in this book is the sixteen-letter viking age futhark. Drawings of individual runes are based on the long-legged runes, also known as normal runes. The reason for this choice is simply that this version was very common just before and after AD 1000 and has gradually become the traditional way of presenting the viking-age runic futhark.

It is beyond the scope and purpose of this book to go into much detail about the development of the runes over the centuries. However, a short list of some of the variations of the futhark is given in an appendix, along with a bibliography for readers who would like to find out more about runes.

The Futhark

The futhark is normally divided into three groups,
each forming an aett (family) which is named after
the first letter. Group one is called Frey's aett, the
second group called Hagal's aett[1] and the last group
Tyr's aett.[2]

Frey's aett	ᚠ ᚢ ᚦ ᚬ ᚱ ᚴ	
	f u þ o r k	
Hagal's aett	ᚼ ᚾ ᛁ ᛆ ᛋ	
	h n i a s	
Tyr's aett	ᛏ ᛒ ᛘ ᛚ ᛦ	
	t b m l R	

Interpreting the Runes

It is quite impossible to assign a runic letter an
equivalent in our modern alphabet. Not only did
the runic alphabet itself vary greatly over the ages,
but languages have also undergone major changes
from the age of the vikings to the present day. We
can only attempt a vague approximation towards an
imaginary normalization. Spelling was not standard-

ized in the heyday of the runes and there was no central authority to issue rules for spelling or guidelines for the use of language. Spelling therefore varied from one country to another, from one runemaster to another, and from one period to the next.

Name	Rune	Modern equivalent
Fe	ᚠ	f, v
Ur	ᚢ	u, o, v, y
Thurs	ᚦ	th
As	ᚬ	o, a, e
Reid	ᚱ	r
Kaun	ᚴ	k, g, nk, ng
Hagal	ᚼ	h, g
Naud	ᚾ	n
Is	ᛁ	i, e, y, j
Ar	ᛅ	a
Sol	ᛋ	s
Tyr	ᛏ	t, d, nt, nd
Bjarkan	ᛒ	b, p, mp, mb
Madur	ᛘ	m
Logur	ᛚ	l
Yr	ᛦ	y, R

It is quite obvious from this list how many permutations are possible in interpreting an old alphabet, not to mention when the language in question has also changed dramatically. However, the list sheds enough light on the matter to give the interested reader the general picture. Similarly, the short history of runes at the end of the book summarizes some of the main variations in form and is designed not as an exhaustive survey or to advance any theory, but merely to give some idea of the richness of the culture in which the runes evolved.

The Runic Poems

Three basic runic poems are known, although they come in a myriad of variations. One is printed here in an English translation. It should be helpful for readers who want to learn the runic alphabet, and hopefully be of general interest as well. As it happens, the runic poems themselves were quite probably meant to be an aid for learning the runes. They might also simply have been riddles, a game to play during the long winter nights.

Two of the runic poems are Scandinavian and one is English. All the poems are structured in the same way, which has led some people to believe that they had some common origin in the distant past, long before AD 1000. In all of them, the name of each rune is rewritten two or three times in the form of a riddle (kenning). In order to understand the name of the rune, the reader or listener has to solve the riddle.

The runic poem printed here (sometimes called the Icelandic rune poem), was tailored to the viking-age futhark. It has sixteen strophes, one for each of the letters of the viking futhark around AD 1000. The oldest manuscript is from the fifteenth century.[3] By that time, many new letters had been added to the runic alphabet. The poem itself only mentions the letters in the old viking futhark. This, among many other things, has given reason to believe that the poem itself is contemporary with the viking futhark.

A second runic poem is sometimes called the Norwegian runic poem, mainly because of the spelling in the oldest manuscript, which dates from the 13th century. Like the first poem, however, it is quite possibly much older. These two poems are very similar. The first line is more often than not the same, and both are tailored to the sixteen-letter viking-age futhark.

It should be pointed out that there is no evidence to prove that the "Norwegian poem" is Norwegian or that the "Icelandic poem" is Icelandic. These names simply spring from the respective spellings in the oldest manuscripts.

The third runic poem is the Anglo-Saxon one and differs from the other two in many ways. It was based on the Anglo-Saxon runic alphabet, which by the time the oldest version of this poem was written was already quite different from the futhark of the vikings. A case has been made for all three poems having a common source.[4]

Neither the Anglo-Saxon nor the Norwegian poem is printed here. The Anglo-Saxon poem is beyond the scope of this book and the Norwegian poem is shorter than the Icelandic one but at the same time so similar that it does not add anything at all.

Other poems are often mentioned in this context, for example the Runatal ("Tally of Runes") in the viking-age Eddic poem Havamal. This is sometimes interpreted as containing a description of the magic qualities of specific runes, although it does not actually mention which ones are being referred to. It is just as likely that the Runatal is referring to magic runes as to alphabetical ones. But the runes of the futhark are not magic runes and have nothing to do with sorcery. The suncross, the wolfcross, the fylfot, etc. are examples of magic runes that have been used by sorcerers through the ages, for completely different purposes.

Another poem from the viking age (also in the Edda), known as Sigurdrifumal, mentions runes quite often. While it describes various categories such as Victory runes, Mind runes, Ale runes and Help runes, it only refers to a few from the futhark by name (Naud = Despair is one example). It is therefore not certain whether the poem refers to letters of the futhark or some kind of magical symbols. Furthermore, runes are widely mentioned in viking-age literature.

Rune stone (Uppland, Sweden)

Rune stone (Uppland, Sweden)

The Names of the Runes

The following section presents the runic alphabet of
the viking age, the sixteen-letter futhark, in a
normalized version, and a runic poem originating in
the viking age. Each strophe opens with the name of
a rune, and in the following three lines its name is
restated in the form of a riddle.[5]

Possibly, this old poem was used as a game. The
teller or reader of the riddle would have omitted the
name of the rune in question, leaving it up to the
listener to guess it.

What is the sitter's joy, a swift journey and the
steed's toil? Answer: the rune *Reid* (Riding).

What is the bark of rivers, the wave's roof and the
doomed man's undoing? Answer: *Is* (Ice).

Whether this poem is a learning aid or a riddle,
or both, these strophes have survived through
centuries and been the source of entertainment and
education for ordinary people, long after the Roman
alphabet had become universal.

Wealth is kinsmen's contention
the sea's flame
and the slitherer's track

slitherer: lit. grave-fish, i.e. serpent.
The serpent Fafnir guarded the treasure hoard of the Niflungs.
Sea's flame is also a kenning for gold.

The rune **Fe** = Wealth

Modern equivalent **f**

Variant ᚡ

Shower is the clouds' weeping
the hay's ruin
and the shepherd's hate

ᚢ

The rune **Ur** = Shower[6]

Modern equivalents **u**, v, o, y

Variants ᚢ h

Giant is woe to women
the cliff-dweller
and death-knower's husband[7]

The rune **Þurs** (Thurs) = Giant

Modern equivalent **th**
Variants Ð Ð Þ

God is an ancient ruler
the king of Asgard
and lord of Valhalla

The rune **As** = God

Modern equivalents **a**, o, a, e
Variants ᚪ ᚠ ᚠ ᚤ ᚥ ᚡ ᚤ

Riding is the sitter's joy
a swift journey
and the steed's toil

The rune **Reid** = Riding

Modern equivalent **r**
Variants R R

Scar is the children's scourge
the battle's mark
and canker's seat

The rune **Kaun** = Scar

Modern equivalents **k**, g, nk, ng
Variants ᚴ ᚼ

Hail is a crystal of cold
a shower of sleet
and the serpents' onslaught

The rune **Hagal** = Hail

Modern equivalents **h**, g
Variants ✳ † †

Need is the servant's grief
a burdensome lot
and soaking work

Need: with a sense of being forced to do something
(the original sense of "bondage", cf. the bondswoman
whose tasks are described here).

The rune **Naud** = Need

Modern equivalent **n**
Variant ᚠ

Ice is the bark of rivers
the wave's roof
and the doomed man's undoing

The rune **Is** = Ice

Modern equivalents **i**, e, y, j

Plenty is men's blessing
a good summer
and a richly grown field

The rune **Ar** = Plenty

Modern equivalent **a**
Variant ↑

Sun is the clouds' shield
a shining crown
and an end to ice's life

The rune **Sol** = Sun

Modern equivalent **s**
Variants ᛁ ᚼ ᛁ

Tyr is a one-handed god
the wolf's leavings
and the king of temples

The god Tyr, whose name is still preserved in the word
Tuesday and is cognate with the Greek Zeus, gave (and lost)
his hand as a pledge when the gods made a fetter to bind the wolf
Fenrir, hence the designation "the wolf's leavings", i.e.
the rest of him that the wolf did not eat.

The rune Tyr

Modern equivalents **t**, d, nt, nd
Variant 1

Birch is a leafy twig
a little tree
and youthful wood

The rune **Bjarkan**[8] = Birch

Modern equivalents b, p, mp, mb
Variants ᛒ ᛔ ᛏ B

Man is man's delight
the earth's increaser
and adorner of ships

Man is man's delight: this phrase is found in Havamal,
"The Sayings of the High One."

The rune **Madur** = Man

Modern equivalent **m**
Variants ↑ ↑ Ψ φ

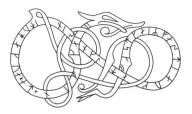

Water is a swirling stream
a wide hot spring
and the ground of fish

The rune **Logur** = Water

Modern equivalent **l**

Yew is a bent bow
brittle iron
and the giant's dart

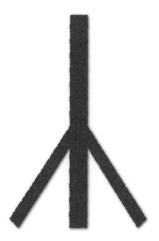

The rune Yr = Yew[9]

Modern equivalents **y**, r
Variants ı ⼂

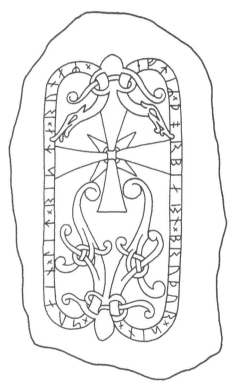

Rune stone (Uppland, Sweden)

The History of Runes

Mythology

Most ancient nations created their own myths about
the origin of writing. The Babylonian god of Fate,
Nebo, was said to have invented the art of writing.
The Egyptians thought that Thot, the great magi-
cian, had made the letters; the Romans were con-
vinced that Mercury had a hand in the making of
the alphabet, while the Jews were of the opinion
that Moses had been the first man to write. The
Greeks taught that the alphabet was derived from
the Phoenicians with a little help from the god
Hermes. An Irish legend tells us that Ogma, the
great god of culture and poetry, invented the Irish
alphabet Ogham.

The Scandinavian version was that Odin created
the alphabet, the futhark. This is stated in many
strophes in the old Eddic poem, Havamal.

> It has been shown
> that if you ask of the runes
> given by the mighty gods
> and painted by the awesome sage,
> it is best to stay silent …

awesome sage: Odin

Runes you will find
and knowable letters,
very great letters
very firm letters
that the awesome sage painted
and the mighty gods made
and the hailer-god carved.

hailer-god: Odin

Or as it says on the Noleby stone in West Gotland in Sweden: "I carved the runes, those which came from the gods".

The Noleby stone

Even in our modern age of scientific fact, the ingenuity of such myths and legends has lost none of its appeal.

The Beginning

Most runologists and historians are of the opinion that runes were first used some time after the birth of Christ.

It is also thought likely that the runic alphabet developed from a mixture of the Greek, Roman and Etruscan alphabets.[10] However, it is impossible to reconstruct exactly how that happened.

Archaeological evidence proves that runes were carved around AD 200 in continental Europe, south of the Nordic countries, and that they were in use in central and northern Europe for at least two or three hundred years. In Britain, runes achieved some currency during the viking age, well into the eleventh century and maybe even longer.

Runes were used throughout the lands dominated by the Scandinavians into the thirteeth century. And in Scandinavia itself, there is evidence of extensive use of runes well into the fourteenth century. After that their use dwindled, but knowledge of them never died out completely, at least not in some areas in Scandinavia.

Rune stone (Gotland, Sweden)

The Futhark

The runic alphabet was called the futhark, after the first six letters.

F U Þ A R K
ᚠ ᚢ ᚦ ᚨ ᚱ ᚲ

It does not take much exercise of the imagination to see the likeness to Roman letters. However, obvious as the links may be, we do not know how to explain them exactly.

In Scandinavia, there have been two futharks: The Old Futhark, which contains 24 letters, and the Young Futhark, which has 16 letters. The Young Futhark used here is normalized and simplified. We have tried to approximate what has been called the normal runes. This is necessary because the futhark exists in many variations and some letters occur in many different forms. For the sake of comprehensibility, we use a standardized version throughout this book.

ᚠᚢᚦᚨᚱᚴ ᚼᚾᛁᛆᛌ ᛐᛒᛘᛦ

f u þ a r k   h n i a s   t b m i R

On page 58 there is an overview of the main variants of the futhark. The transliteration into Roman letters given here is also simplified (and therefore misleading, of course). For example, the ᚠ rune was used to designate both k and g; the ↑ sign meant both t and d; and ⋏ designated sounds that changed drastically during the four hundred years that passed from the time when the sixteen-letter futhark came into being until new letters were added to it.

Christianity

During the fourth century and through the sixth, the old futhark was used throughout central Europe and in Britain and Scandinavia. The young futhark apparently replaced it during the seventh and eighth centuries. It seems that the old futhark was replaced on the one hand with the Roman alphabet in central Europe, and on the other hand with the shorter sixteen-letter futhark in the still heathen Scandinavia. Quite possibly, the spread of Christianity influenced the change in the futhark from 24 letters to 16. Christianity brought the Roman alphabet, which as its name suggests was primarily used for writing in Latin. In Britain, the futhark developed independently and many letters were added as time went by. The Anglo-Saxon futhark diverged quite early on from the one used in Scandinavia.

The Danes were christianized long before Christianity reached Norway and Sweden. It seems that the use of runes declined earlier in Denmark than in, for instance, Sweden.

From 24 letters to 16 letters

One reason for reducing the number of letters in the futhark in the beginning of the ninth century may have been that the sixteen-letter alphabet was better suited for expressing the sounds of the language spoken in Scandinavia than the twenty-four letters that preceded it. This may be related to the changes that were taking place in the Germanic languages in that period.[11]

It is also possible that these changes were simply necessary because the older futhark arose from a language so different from the one spoken in England and Scandinavia that the alphabet had to be adapted anew. It is striking, however, that this drastic change took place fairly consistently throughout the Scandinavian world.

Letters reintroduced

As time went by, the futhark underwent many changes. In the late viking age in the latter half of the tenth century, new letters were added to the Scandinavian futhark. The sixteen-letter futhark had proven to be inadequate. For example: The same letter was used to designate k and g, and there was great difficulty in distinguishing between some vocals. The word dreng- (meaning man or an honourable man) could well be spelled ᛏᚱᛁᚴ, namely **trik** (it was not always the custom to put n before g or k); a word like Gunnar (a common personal name) could well be written ᚴᚢᚾᛅᚱ, namely **kunar** (double consonants would normally not be written as such, and no distinction was ever made between miniscule and capital letters).

The Scandinavian languages were developing quickly, and the alphabet had to follow suit. Among the changes was the addition of a dot to an existing letter to change its value.

Example: ᛒ designated either b or p and to distinguish between the two, a new letter was made, the letter ᛔ which designates p. Another example: ᚴ could mean either k or g. To make a clear difference between k and g, the ᚴ rune was dotted and the letter ᚵ came into being, designating g.

In Iceland, learned essays were written in the twelfth and thirteenth century on the problems of adapting the Roman alphabet to the Icelandic language,[12] and also about how to amend the runic alphabet.

Variants of Runes

1 Normal runes

ᚠᚢᚦᚨᚱᚴ ᚼᚾᛁᛅᛋ ᛏᛒᛘᛚᛦ
f u þ a r k h n i a s   t b m l R

2 Short-legged runes

ᚠᚢᚦᛂᚱᚴ ᚼᚾᛁᛀ ' ᛏᚠᛁᛐᵢ
f u þ a r k h n i a s   t b m l R

3 Legless runes or Helsing runes

f u þ o r k h n i a s   t b m l R

Bibliography

Dickins, B. *Runic and Heroic Poems of the Old Teutonic Peoples.* Cambridge 1915

Page, R.I. *Runes and Runic Inscriptions.* Woodbridge 1995

Page, R.I. *Reading the Past: Runes.* London 1987

Page, R.I. *The Icelandic Rune-Poem.* London 1999

Barnes, Hagland and Page, *The Runic Inscriptions of Viking Age Dublin.* Dublin 1997

Arntz, H. *Handbuch der Runenkunde.* Halle 1944

Bæksted, A. *Målruner og Troldruner.* Copenhagen 1952

Kulturhistorisk Leksikon for nordisk middelalder. Copenhagen 1969
    Article by Aslak Liestøl

Hávamál og Völuspá. Svart á hvítu, Reykjavík 1987

A.G. Smith, *Viking Designs.* New York, 1999

Åke Ohlmarks, *Fornnordiskt Lexikon.* Stockholm 1994

Runmärkt. Ed. Solbritt Benneth et. al., Carlsons, Stockholm 1994
    Articles by: Þórgunnur Snædal, Rune Palm, Lena Peterson, Terje
    Spurkland, Jan Ragnar Hagland, Ingrid Sannes Johnsen, James E.
    Knirk.

Þórgunnur Snædal, *Íslenskar rúnir í norrænu ljósi,* Árbók hins íslenska
    fornleifafélags, Reykjavík 1998

Francois Xavier Dillmann, *Um rúnir í íslenskum fornbókmenntum,* Skírnir,
    Reykjavík 2000

Einar Ólafur Sveinsson, *Íslenzkar bókmenntir í fornöld,* Reykjavík 1962

Jan Ragnar Hagland: *Møte mellom to skriftspråkskulturar?* Til spørsmålet om
    runeskrift har noko å seia for lingvistisk analyse i Første grammatiske
    avhandling.Íslenskt mál og almenn málfræði, vol. 15, Reykjavík 1993

Notes

[1.] In old Norse, aett means "kin" or "clan". As the word "aett" is similar to
"atta" which means "eight", and there are eight letters in each group,
some people believe that originally "aett" was to have been understood
as "eight".

[2.] It should be underlined here that we have chosen to present a very
simplified futhark. Several questions arise concerning this table, e.g.
whether ᚼ should turn right or left; whether ᛏ has a whole hat or just
half, how the ᛙ should turn (ᛙ or ᛨ), whether this version should use ᛁ
for s, which of the many variations of ᚦ should be used, etc. Definite
forms are impossible to establish for some of the runes. One example is
the fourth rune: ᚬ . This is just as often written ᚭ, at least in Norway.
Even though the futhark printed in this edition is known as "normal
runes" or "long runes", the version given in the appendix (the short-
legged runes) is just as "normal" or common, judging by archaeological
evidence. And it is of course possible that future archaeological findings
will change the picture. The alphabet printed in this book is therefore
inevitably a compromise chosen from several possibilities.

[3.] AM. 687, 4to

[4.] B. Dickins, 1915, p. 6

[5.] In his book The Icelandic Rune Poem, R.I. Page concludes that it is
impossible to reconstruct a hypothetical "definitive" text of the poem,
but maps the problems that bar the way.

[6.] Shower: an earlier rune, signifying ox or aurochs, has apparently become
confused with a similar-sounding word meaning light rain, drizzle.

[7.] Death-knower's husband: conjectural, a literal rendition of R.I. Page's
new reading here of the name Valrún. This translation sidesteps a
tautology, since the meaning is ogress, trollwoman.

[8.] According to Aslak Liestøl (see bibliography), the meaning of the word
Bjarkan is uncertain, but it is translated here as a cognate of Björk,
"birch."

[9.] Yew: translated as such here simply to supply a word for the rune; its
original sense is unknown. There is an obvious clash of meaning
between "bent bow" and "brittle iron" no matter how this is translated.
Two similar words, meanings or rune traditions have presumably merged
at some point to produce this irresolvable verse.

[10.] The Etruscans lived in northern Italy.

[11.] Among other things, the umlaut shift.

[12.] See for example the sources named in: Jan Ragnar Hagland, Reykjavík
1993, pp. 159-173.